To
_____

From
_____

Date
_____

I Just Can't Take It Anymore!

Text Copyright © 2012 by Anthony DeStefano
Photos compiled by Anthony DeStefano

Published by Harvest House Publishers
Eugene, Oregon 97402
www.harvesthousepublishers.com

ISBN 978-0-7369-4854-8

Published in association with PMA Literary & Film Management, Inc.

Design and production by Garborg Design Works, Savage, Minnesota

Photographs used with permission from the following sources:
iStockPhoto: pages 3,5,6,8,9,11,16,17,19,22,25,26,30,31,32,33,34,36,40,42,43,44,46,48,49,52,53,
55,57,61,63
Inmagine: pages 1,11,12,15,20,21,23,24,27,29,35,37,40,41,47,50,54,56,58,60,61,62,64
Getty Images: pages 32,59
Lina Shuster, Lasting Memories Photography: pages 18,51
Curt Ciumei: pages 5,10,39,53,63
Shiloah Horn: pages 4,7,28
Colleen Eronson: pages 8,38,45
Rob Wilson: pages 13,14

Digital photo editing by Schmalen Design,Inc.

Printed in China

13 14 15 16 17 18 / FC / 10 9 8 7 6 5 4

I Just Can't Take It Anymore!

ANTHONY DeSTEFANO

HARVEST HOUSE PUBLISHERS
EUGENE, OREGON

Dedicated to

Kimberly,

whose courageous,

humorous, and

faith-filled response

to suffering inspired

this book.

Sometimes I just don't understand life.

I've heard that God only gives you what you can handle.

But if that's true, He must have me
confused with somebody else...

because I JUST CAN'T TAKE IT ANYMORE!

I hate my job.

I have a knack for making the wrong business decisions.

I have the most horrible hair days.

For some reason I can't lose weight.

I seem to make a habit out of getting involved
in the wrong relationships.

Everyone has abandoned me.

Even my pet died!

My life is just one big mess!

I'm so tired of dealing with problems... I just want to get into bed, pull up the covers, and sleep, sleep, sleep.

Sometimes I wonder if God is really up there or—
even worse—if He just doesn't care.

But down deep, I know that can't be true because life can be so beautiful too.

After all, there's music

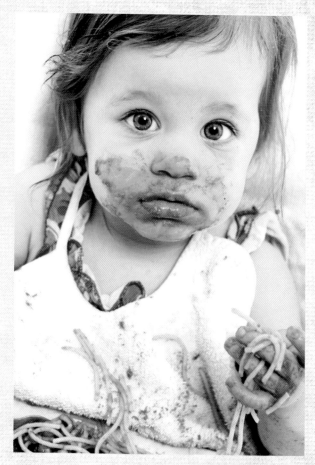

and good food

and good books

and puppies

and Christmas

and romance

and just being alive!

So what's the answer to this mystery?

If life's so great and God loves me so much,
why do I always feel like my heart is breaking?

Why do I feel SO BAD?

I wonder... Is God trying to test me?
Because if He is, it would be nice if He could
make the tests a little bit easier.

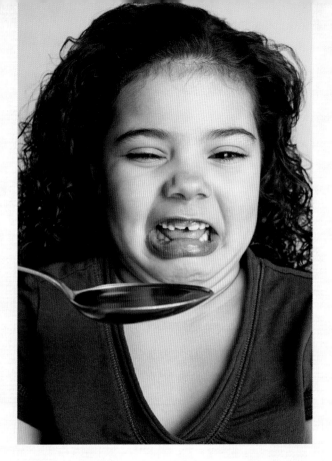

Is He trying to cure me of some problem I have?
Because if He is, I wish the medicine
He's giving me wasn't so hard to swallow.

Is it that we're all connected somehow and God wants to use my pain to help others who are hurting?

Because right now I could sure use some TLC myself!

Is it that God wants to build my character
and make me brave, strong, and smart?

Because you know I wouldn't mind being weak and stupid—
at least once in a while!

Or is it, maybe, that God wants me to stop ignoring Him and start paying attention to the things that really matter in life?

Like praying more…

helping those less fortunate than me...

saying sorry for the things I've done wrong—
as well as forgiving the people who have hurt me...

forgiving myself too for the mistakes I've made along the way (and God knows there have been some doozies!)...

and standing up for what's right in the world!

Because if God really wants me to do those things,
I'll try my best to start right now.

But then again, maybe God has something else in mind.
Maybe there's a bigger plan I can't see.

After all, I've noticed that the bad things that happen in life often lead to something good—

that the scariest storms...

often turn into the most glorious skies,

that the seeds we bury in the ground...

often come to life in the most extraordinary ways,

and that even the toughest experiences...

can result in miracles.

In fact, I seem to remember that God went through some pretty tough times too—maybe even worse than mine.

But somehow, some way, He was able to come through
everything okay and transform even the most terrible suffering

into the happiest ending.

If He can do THAT, then maybe He's got
something special planned for me too.

Maybe if I just give it a little more time, I'll see that something wonderful is right around the corner.

So I guess the best thing for me to do is try not to despair...

or be too grumpy...

or get too worried about things I can't change...

and just take a deep breath,

go one step at a time,

work up the courage to do the things I KNOW I have to do,

try to find a couple of good friends to confide in and maybe even lend a hand (because no one can bear the burden of life's troubles alone),

and have a little faith that the One who made the universe
and set the stars and planets in motion

can help me figure a way to get through all my problems

no matter how overwhelming they may seem now.

If only I put my trust in Him...

The end.